Judy's

You Just Can't Make This Stuff Up

Judy S. Walter

Layout and Design by
Penny Maxson

Printed in the USA

Copyright 2018 by Judy S. Walter

All Rights Reserved

ISBN-13: 978-1727706048
ISBN-10: 1727706048

Cover photo by Penny Maxson

Unknowingly, my daughter Heather gave me the title for this book after reading the first two essays. This book is dedicated to her.

Contents

Purpose
Lunch in Old Town Scottsdale
Power Struggle
What a Day!
Mammogram
Bridges
Vet Appointment
Age
Misunderstanding
The Students
No Idea
Confused Teacher
Quiet
Coffee or Tea
Sugar Bowl
A Day at the Restaurant
Panic Attack
Turkey
Clothes
I Can't Be Trusted with Cheese
Discount Flight
Socks
Staples

Contents Cont'd

Sylvia's Confusion
Pillow cases
Birds
Salt Caves
Underwear
Summer Funds
Inspired
Responsibility and Consequences
Toe
Eyeglass Cases
Water and Blood Work
Again with the Blood Work
How to Waste Time
Trip to the Market
Centralia Outlets
Coffee at 3 AM
Old School
Drug Costs
How Rumors Get Started
Hot Dogs
About the Author
Book List

Purpose

My best friend types my books. Yes, I hand write. I can't compose more than an email at the computer. Don't laugh. We are all different.

After reading my second book in this series, she asked me what the purpose of the book was. Duh, humor. Most of the essays are written to poke fun at the human condition and make people laugh.

At such a violent time in American history, who doesn't need an escape and a few laughs? I mean really. The news is depressing.

My first book of humor was <u>Memories of a High School Teacher</u>. It was not meant to chronicle my short teaching career. It was written to make people laugh.

I've had to deal with a lot of negative and traumatic stuff in my life. In all cases, three things got me through all and helped me survive: caring people, my faith, and my sense of humor. My mother and my Uncle Bob both had a tremendous sense of humor. My father did also, but he was only in my life briefly.

So, I think I inherited my sense of humor. I believe it is genetic. As a baby and young child, my daughter had a tremendous sense of humor. I used to joke that she would grow up to be a clown. That didn't happen.

A few essays are social commentary. Hopefully, they will cause you to think and look at the world from a new prospective. Most poke fun at the human condition. I doubt you'll roll on the floor laughing, but this book should give you a few chuckles.

Lunch in Old Town Scottsdale

Mom wanted to go to Old Town, Scottsdale. She wanted to buy some gifts to take home to Cindy for cat sitting and Penny, her best friend who is her airport taxi and part time cat sitter. Mom and I also found a 1950's diner, Sugar Bowl, we both liked for lunch.

The first time we ate there, we had a corner booth that was uncomfortable for me. This time we were seated at a table by the window facing the street. The sidewalk was literally on the other side of the window.

Well, Mom has ruined a number of sweatshirts, T-shirts, and blouses over the years from spilling food down the front. Lately, she has taken to wearing a napkin as a bib in restaurants. It doesn't matter whom she is with or how classy the restaurant is, she tucks her napkin in her collar. No embarrassment. No shame. I've gotten used to it.

The waitress brought our turkey dinners and you guessed. She asked for more napkins and used one as a bib. There we sat in the window for all passersby to see.

The first couple walked by, looked at Mom, and started laughing. We figured it out instantly. Mom and I laughed so hard we could hardly eat.

Another couple walked by and reacted the same way. I said, "They're probably saying, 'Look at that crazy old lady.' " Mom has white hair. We laughed some more. Mom took the whole thing with her normal sense of humor. At least she didn't ruin her red T-shirt.

From Heather's Perspective

Power Struggle

About six months ago my daughter and her husband got a Yorkie puppy. At that time their menagerie consisted of a white lab, a black rescue that is a lab mix, and two white Maltese - a female and her younger brother. The white male lab had assumed the position of alpha male.

Because of my daughter's allergies, it became necessary to find a new home for the white lab. That was accomplished with a friend adopting him.

Let me give you some history of the dogs. Heather and her husband were living in Washington state when she found Bailey, the lab rescue. Bailey is a sweetheart. She's older now.

Next her husband came home with a precious Maltese puppy – Daisy. Heather became very attached to her new puppy.

Eventually her husband wanted a puppy to bond with him, so he brought home Wally, Daisy's half-brother, For the first two weeks, Heather took him to work with her. Now, he's attached to her.

Time went by and her husband wanted the white lab puppy. He grew into the alpha dog.

The dogs all knew their places.

More time went by and they moved. Then one day Heather's husband saw a Yorkie puppy online and fell in love with him. They contacted the breeder and when the Yorkie was old enough, he joined the motley crew.

The white lab was still the alpha dog. Heather's asthma and allergies worsened, and they decided to find a new home for him. A friend had recently lost one of her dogs to cancer and was willing to take him. Recent pictures show a happy dog in his new home.

The absence of the white lab disrupted the balance of power among the dogs. Wally has been trying to assert himself as the alpha dog. Buddy the Yorkie wants to play and Wally growls. There is much growling over everything including food and toys.

Wally has developed other bad behaviors. He recently peed in Buddy's food dish. Today we found poop on Buddy's back. Yuck.

Buddy has his own strange behaviors. The other day he followed Bailey outside and stood under her while she peed. Heather had to take Buddy upstairs and put him in the tub and give him a bath. All of the other dogs stood by the tub and watched. Bailey and Wally thought she was trying to drown Buddy. It was pathetic to watch, but Buddy sure smelled better afterwards.

Wally seemed apologetic at the time, but that didn't last. Remember the poop on Buddy's back? Where do you think that came from? And, of course, Wally is back to growling.

What a Day!

What a day! To begin with, I was late paying my TV cable bill. I meant to call and get an extension yesterday. Forgot. So, this morning they shut it off. So I had to deal with that.

Next, I stopped at my chiropractor's office. It's just up the street from my house. I haven't been there for a while. It's hard for me to call when they're open during the school hours. And the hours keep changing.

I was told that since it was over six months since I had been there, I would have to pay $75 for a re-evaluation. Medicare doesn't pay, so it would be out of my pocket. I told the girl I didn't think so and I left. What a rip off. My cardiologist doesn't do that. My family practitioner doesn't do that.

Oh, the day keeps getting better. I went to Fayetteville to check my P.O. box. Again, I had not been there in quite a while. I really don't get anything but junk mail there anymore.

There was an invoice for my box due in April. I went to the window to see if I had paid it. No. The woman told me it had been closed. Again, why should I pay for something I no longer use, so I told her to keep it closed. That is $60 a year I won't have to pay.

But this chiropractor thing bugs me. I think I'll go back and ask to talk to him in person. Wish me luck.

Mammogram

I must admit, I'm not very faithful in getting these things done. Actually, I hate having them done so much so, that several years go by before I decide to have one done.

The last time I was at my doctor's, she asked if I would consider having one. I said maybe, so she gave me the paper. She also sent the request to the facility. Someone later called me. I said I would schedule it when I had the time.

One day I felt brave and went to the Rhonda Brake Shreiner Women's Center and scheduled it. I could still back out.

The day of the mammogram arrived, and I kept my appointment. I am over weight and find the exam very painful. Well, the technician squished my breasts on the equipment, and I ouched around. I asked her if everyone was so sensitive. She gave me an affirmative answer. Probably just trying to console me. Either it really hurt or I'm a big baby.

After it was over I got dressed and left. As I walked through the waiting room, she and the receptionist were standing at the desk looking at me rather pitifully. Great. Something must have shown on the x-ray, I thought.

A day or two later, I was able to log into the website and get my report. Something did show: fat. Breast composition: fat. The report said my breasts are almost entirely fat.

I've never read that before. No wonder those women looked at me pitifully.

On another note, I am thankful the report was negative. Just fat breasts.

Bridges

Did I tell you I'm afraid of bridges? When I'm traveling with my friend Penny and we encounter a bridge, I just close my eyes. She thinks I'm a sissy, but the fear is real.

Years ago, daughter Heather and I went to San Diego. At one point I was driving when we came upon that long causeway to Coronado. There was no place to pull over and change drivers. I had to keep going. My hands gripped the steering wheel so tightly I was afraid I would pull it off the steering column. I was also afraid I couldn't drive straight and would wreck the car or go into the ocean.

Well, we made it. I did not have a heart attack or die of fright. Almost. We enjoyed our stay on Coronado. Actually, we met a friend of Heather's and decided to go into Mexico. Her friend drove.

I have good memories of Mexico, but I'll leave those for another time. We returned to the friend's house and retrieved our SUV. Heather drove. As we were on the causeway, I looked over at her. She was staring straight ahead and had a death grip on the steering wheel. I didn't say a word – just prayed.

By the way, we're taking that same trip for my seventieth birthday. Guess who's driving across the causeway?

Vet Appointment

Last week Mitzi had an appointment for her yearly checkup. I debated making the appointment since she had been there twice in the spring for IBD, but I had some questions for the vet.

Her appointment was 10:20 on Thursday. At 9:30 I put her carrier in the dining room. Usually, she just walks in. Well, I guess the two visits in the spring did her in.

Let me tell you this. When a fifteen pound opinionated, part Maine Coon female cat doesn't want to do something, she isn't doing it. Period.

I finally took the roof off her carrier and plopped her in it and quickly tried to replace the roof. Her door had come off. I replaced it, but the handle was on the inside and I couldn't get the front latched. Out came a front paw. They are large, I might add. I tried to pick the carrier up, and out came her head. So that didn't work.

I have two other carriers, so I tried the soft one. Forget it. She has never gone in it and today was not an exception.

Next, I went into the garage and got the larger sturdy carrier that I bought from a cat breeder. Mitzi has used it a couple of times. I prefer not to use it because it is heavier for me to carry.

I rounded her up and attempted to put her into this carrier. No way. Her mind was made up. She knew going into the carrier meant a trip to the vet and she was having no part of it.

By this time, I was worn out and sweating. It was now 10:00 and her appointment was in twenty minutes, a fifteen to twenty minute drive. Mitzi went behind the couch and I picked up my purse and left.

So, you see, I had a vet appointment. When I showed up alone the vet just laughed. She did not weigh or examine me, but I got flea medicine and my other questions answered.

Mitzi

Age

I am a substitute teacher in the local school district. This morning as I was walking down the hallway of the high school, I heard two teachers whom I know discussing age and the one's mother. Something was said about being over seventy. So, I stopped and waited for them.

The one was talking about all the things her eighty-six year old mother does. She drives people to and from church. Now she thinks she wants to start a grief support group. Her daughter told her she is way busier than she is.

The kids are also concerned about her driving. Then there is the concern that one of her elderly passengers could fall and they would both be on the ground.

The other teacher thought all her involvements in life is what keeps her going. I listened with fascination. I, too, applaud the woman's activity. We can't just stop living because we reach a certain age.

When their conversation seemed to wind down, I mentioned that I had heard them say something about being over seventy. Then came the shocker. I told them I am turning seventy this year. Watching their reactions and hearing their comments was priceless.

Misunderstanding

I think my daughter probably thinks I am developing dementia. Twice recently she says I have misunderstood what she has told me. Hmmm.

The most recent time actually benefited a former student – now aged 55. I'll tell you about that later. First the misunderstanding.

On Monday I was driving to my best friend's house after school when my cell phone rang. It was Heather.

First a little background. On Saturday, the mass shooting had taken place at an outdoor concert in Las Vegas. OK, are you with me so far?

She makes remarks about not hearing from me and my not saying anything on Facebook. She thought I must not know. She mentions the shooting in Vegas. She then proceeds to tell me that she and her husband were supposed to be there, but they had to cancel because he got sick.

I almost wrecked my car. I cannot begin to tell you how I felt.

She then told me they were supposed to meet friends there. They had spoken with them, and they were fine.

I was still in a state of shock when I walked into Penny's house. She knew about it because she had seen the post on Facebook.

Now to tell you how my supposed misunderstanding benefitted the lady I ran into at Giant last night. She was in a funk over some personal issues. I listened. She was sad. Then I told her I was thankful and why. My story made her day. She was so glad for good news for a change. So, you see, sometimes not getting the message right can be a good thing.

It turns out that my daughter and husband were supposed to be in Vegas but not where the shooting took place. I got lost somewhere in the conversation.

The Students

A girl drops her books onto the floor. They had been sitting on her desk. She asks the boy across from her to pick them up. He ignores her. Other students step over them. She complains that no one will pick them up.

The boy sitting in front of me has ear phones playing music. His head bops around while he stares at the other students. He's done very little work.

When I took attendance, a boy complained because I could not remember how to pronounce his name. He said I'd been his sub probably twenty times. He has an attitude, so I ignore him.

Several students have cups of coffee or tea. They are ninth graders.

Now the pencil sharpener doesn't work. A girl says it needs batteries. I do not have batteries. Someone fixes it. The girl then proceeds to use it for five minutes. Now the pencil is an inch long.

The boy who gave me the most trouble at the beginning of the period is now working. Oh, wait. He just took a music break.

A few students are working quietly. God bless them. They are not needy.

It's now the next period. Most of these kids are tenth graders and better behaved. A girl just spilled her bottle of water and ruined her paper as well as those of nearby students. Guess I spoke too soon.

The next class is larger, and there are not enough bottles of glue for each group to have one. So, I have to be the glue police. Some students are OK with giving up a bottle of glue; some question why. The teacher should have provided more.

I started this essay in order to mentally escape from some of the bad behavior of the first period. Maybe I should do what the kids do, and put ear buds in and listen to music.

No Idea

I'd like to write another serious, research based book. I did that the year I retired from full time teaching. It was about the Holocaust. The book still sells for me.

The problem I'm currently experiencing is having an idea or subject I want to research. People have made suggestions, but I have not been struck by any of them.

It also needs to be a subject that others will find interesting, otherwise, no one would buy the book. Such a dilemma.

Now, I have to stop writing this essay and change clothes (get dressed really) to meet a high school friend for lunch. Perhaps she'll have an idea for me. I'd better take a tablet along. Can't trust my memory. I'll let you know if she comes up with anything for me.

Confused Teacher

On the Wednesday before Thanksgiving, I had a sub job scheduled at one of the middle schools. I had taken it more than a month ago. It was an early dismissal day, so it would not have been difficult.

I arrived early as usual. The secretary had my folder ready. I clocked in and went up to the room. The teacher had papers all over her desk, but no lesson plan. Although it was a scheduled absence and not an emergency, I still thought she might have emailed the plans to another teacher.

As I was writing my name on the board, she walked in. She had no idea why I was there. She did not remember putting the absence in the system.

Since she could not get her computer to work, she went down the hall to use another teacher's. I waited. Finally, I walked out in the hall to see what was going on just as her husband (also a teacher) was telling another male teacher about the situation and laughing. I did not find it funny. It was affecting my income, not his.

I asked where she went, and he said she

was down at the office. So I headed that way. As I reached the office, she and one of the principals were walking into the hallway. She was staying, and I had no job.

The secretary called and tried to place me at the high school, but they were covered. I waited while she tried to reach my employer.

Another principal came in and commented on the morning's confusion. I told her I would never sub for this teacher again.

They offered to let me stay and assist the emotional support teacher. I know my limitations. At this point, I needed emotional support. I declined.

Quiet

Have you ever tried to keep a room full of seniors quiet because of state testing in the next room? Most comply.

The two girls sitting next to me talk incessantly. Yes, they whisper, but it is constant. I can't read because it is too much of a distraction.

I'm getting sleepy. I can't drink water because then I will have to pee. There's no one else to watch the students. Also, I can't walk past the barrier on this floor because of the testing.

And the girls continue to talk. Now, I must ask a boy to lower his voice. Five hours and fifteen minutes to go. Will I survive?

I did not know they were testing when I took this job. I thought it would be a regular day with a change in classes and a break. Yes, there will be lunch – an eternity from now.

This is the Career Magnet School. A boy I remember from the high school came in about an hour ago. He was not doing well at the high school and disliked being there. His grades kept him from this school. Somehow, he got to come here this year. He told me it saved him from dropping out.

Five more hours to go. The two girls continue to talk incessantly. I may go crazy.

Coffee or Tea

Have you ever wondered why some people are coffee drinkers and others are tea drinkers? I have.

I love the smell of coffee. When I was eight years old and living in Mass., they made something called Coffee time syrup. You put it in milk. It was delicious.

Hershey's now makes coffee ice cream. I consumed a container in two days. Now that I'm thinking about it, I suppose I'll have to buy some – and another box of Lactaid pills.

Just now a girl came into study hall carrying a large coffee she bought in the coffee shop upstairs. She added packets of sugar to it. When she replaced the lid, the Styrofoam container buckled and spilled. Wow – did it ever smell good. She told me the flavoring was caramel and French vanilla.

I wish I could drink coffee but my stomach revolts. I'm a tea drinker – life long. I wonder if it's in our DNA?

Sugar Bowl

The Sugar Bowl is a fifties style sandwich and ice cream shop. You'll recognize it by its pink colored exterior. Located in Old Town Scottsdale, it is a must visit on your tour of Old Town. It's a perfect place for a sandwich and a milkshake.

They have several tables located right up against the windows for a passerby to watch as you take each bite, drop food onto your clothes, spill your drink, and overall share in your dining experience.

They have a hot meal selection each day of the week. Our favorite is the hot turkey, but it's only served on Tuesdays and Thursdays. We had our hearts set on turkey and gravy, but it was Wednesday.

I don't remember what Heather got, but I ordered a turkey club. It was way too large to bite into. The bread must have passed over the toaster instead of being toasted.

Heather watched me bite into the sandwich only to have it explode on my plate. We laughed loudly as others in the restaurant looked on. The more they looked, the louder we laughed.

Despite the mess and difficulty eating the

sandwich, it was delicious. I would recommend it if you like turkey. Next time I'll have them eliminate the center slice of bread. Maybe it will fit in my mouth then.

A Day at the Restaurant

Some days I have no lunch plans. Sometimes I ask a friend to go to lunch and she says no. Other times I stay home. Then there was yesterday.

Last week I called my friend Sue whom I had not seen in months. She was visiting her daughter and grandchildren, but said she would call and make plans to get together for lunch.

She called on Monday and we made plans to meet at 11:30 on Wednesday at the Capital. I chose a place that I knew would have food I could eat since I'd had three teeth extracted two weeks ago. Good Plan.

Tuesday evening my friend Marie emailed me and said she was going to the Capital at 1:15 on Wednesday and wondered if I could meet her there. Marie teaches piano classes at a music school at Wilson College which is not far from the restaurant.

I said sure and explained that I would already be there and just stay after my first lunch and wait for her. She asked if I was sure I wanted to stay that long. No problem. I always take a book to read.

I arrived early and told Sharon, the waitress,

my plan. No problem. Sue arrived and we ordered. We ate and chatted. I had several glasses of iced tea.

Sue called her daughter to see what time she wanted to meet at the library. We talked some more and then she had to leave.

Well, I had about a half hour to wait. I got out my book and read. Eventually, I got sleepy, so I drank more tea.

Marie showed up about 1:20. She was starved and ordered one of their daily specials – liver and onions with mashed potatoes. I forgot to mention that Sharon was now off for the day and Ruby waited on us.

Marie finally decided to have coffee and I had more iced tea – a couple of times.

Marie had just returned from her grandson's wedding in Japan. She showed me some of the pictures she had on her iPad.

It was 2:40 when we left the restaurant. Marie had to be back for a class at 3:00.

Guess what? I'm meeting two other friends at the Capital today at 1:00. Yesterday I had a hot turkey sandwich. Today I think I'll have a hot roast beef sandwich.

I walked last evening. Better do that again today.

Panic Attack

Do you live on the edge financially? Do you find yourself in a situation where there is more month than money?

It happens to many of us occasionally – to some more often than others. If you fall into the latter category, DO NOT EVER log into your bank account before going to bed.

This is one of the fastest ways I know of to throw yourself into a panic attack. This could keep you up the rest of the night.

If you have a negative balance in your checking account, what are you going to do about it at bedtime, especially if you are broke?

Why torture yourself at bedtime? Wait until morning to do that. Who knows? Maybe with a clear head and a good night's sleep you'll be able to come up with a sensible plan of action. Robbing a bank or standing on a street with a tin cup are not sensible solutions.

Turkey

I had dinner with a friend last Sunday. We live in opposite ends of the county, so we met halfway at a little diner in St. Thomas. They have good food.

We hadn't seen each other for a while so we had lots to talk about. Eventually, she brought up the subject of the cat they had acquired a number of years ago. She talked about how it came to reside on their property. They live in the country – back a lane.

One day the cat stopped eating, so she took it to the vet. They had been feeding it dry cat food. The vet informed her the cat had no teeth and they would have to feed him canned food.
(I forget if it was a male or a female.)

So Dara went out and bought cans of food. That worked for a long time.

One day Dara was at the grocery store and saw they had turkeys on sale for a cheap price, so she bought one. The price per pound was less than she was paying for a can of cat food.

Well, her granddaughter spent the weekend with them. She could smell the turkey roasting and it smelled good. She asked her grandma if they were having it for dinner.

Dara said, "No, honey. That's for the cat."

After it was finished roasting, Dara set it on the counter to cool. Then she went to work pulling all the meat off the bones and put in small bags and froze them.

She did relent and let her granddaughter sample it.

Clothes

I remembered this story while putting socks in the dryer and decided to tell it to you.

A few weeks ago I met two friends for lunch. We met at the Capital. I've known the one just slightly longer than the other, although we don't see each other very often. We all substitute teach.

The one friend – whom we shall call Sylvia – and I often meet after school for tea or a late lunch. Sylvia is always well dressed. Her style is very different from mine. She says it's because she's from the city, and I'm from the country. I think it's just because we're two different people. Also, her husband is a doctor. She can afford style.

In the summer you will typically find me in jeans and a T-shirt. Yes, I go out to eat dressed that way. I figure my money spends the same as that of a well-dressed person. Occasionally, Sylvia will say I dress more casually than she does. Whatever.

About a month ago we were talking on the phone and Sylvia asked me why I didn't wear dresses. She's never seen me in a dress and thought I would look nice in one. Well, let me tell you this. I was in my mid-thirties when I last wore a skirt. This flat butt looks worse in a skirt than in jeans or slacks.

Back to the restaurant. Instead of jeans and a T-shirt, I decided to wear slacks, a polo, and the very nice colorful sweater/jacket my daughter bought me. I thought sure Sylvia would comment on it. NOT a word!

Later, after returning from the restroom, I stopped an front of our table and asked Sylvia what she thought of my new sweater/jacket? I explained that Heather bought it for me. She liked it and thought it looked nice as did the other friend.

We're getting together again on Friday at the same restaurant. I'm wearing jeans and a T-shirt.

I Can't Be Trusted with Cheese

You read the title correctly. It's a fact. I cannot be trusted with cheese. I'm a cheese addict. Did I mention that I'm also lactose intolerant?

They make pills for that. I buy lots of them. I also take Crestor to help unclog my arteries.

Yesterday I went to Sunnyway to buy eggs. I like their eggs. They are local. What happened? You guessed it. A half ring cut of Longhorn cheese jumped into my cart.

I always get a small cart even if I only want one item. My purse needs a place to hang out other than on my shoulder.

I know I said the cheese jumped into my cart when in reality I inspected several before making my selection. But it was Longhorn.

My sinuses hate Longhorn cheese. Just ask them. My taste buds, on the other hand, love Longhorn cheese. I spend money on Lactaid pills just so I can eat Longhorn cheese.

On the way home, I stopped at the Butcher Shoppe. I needed lunch meat from their deli meat and cheese counter. Did I say cheese?

Another favorite is White American cheese. Over the years I've bought different brands. My current favorite is Boars Head. I ordered a half pound sliced. I told the young man to make it a heavy half pound.

It was a delightful evening of eating cheese. I stuck to the White American. No, I'm not racist. I made two grilled cheese sandwiches. One is never enough. And I ate plain slices, all with the help of lots of Lactaid pills.

Do you see how I could save money? If I left the cheese alone, I wouldn't have to buy Lactaid pills. Like that is ever going to happen.

I've been in love with cheese forever. When I was young and we travelled across the country by car, we would stop at roadside cafes, and I would order a cheese sandwich on white bread with butter. Delicious.

At a party, I'm the one who will be hanging out by the cheese plate.

Years ago – many years ago – during the divorce and custody hearings, my then husband testified that I ate cheese knowing it would make me sick. Yes, he did. In open court. (That was before the readily available Lactaid pills.) What an accusation. Bring on the handcuffs.

I try to leave cheese alone. I actually can go periods of time without eating it. Then one day I find myself unhappy because I'm not having an evening snack of cheese. A snack is a quarter to half a pound.

By the way, I only have about three slices left from last night's White American binge.

Discount Flight

Discount airlines. You know who you are. You make it appealing with your cheap tickets. Yes, cheap fares for the flight, so you book it. Then comes the kickers.

Would you like a seat? Yes, please. That will be extra. Now, I understand if there are available free seats, but you want a different one and are willing to pay extra. I've done this on American.

No, there are no free seats. You have to pay. Shouldn't the seat be included in the airfare? What are you supposed to do otherwise – stand in the aisle? No, airplanes don't allow standing. Must be seated for take-off, landing and turbulence.

There is no option but to pay for a seat. The airfare cost $191. I chose a $17 seat. We're up to $208 now. I can add or use a calculator.

Now for the next shocker. I am only allowed to take my purse free. I carry a rather large shoulder bag. I had to measure it to make sure it met the size requirements. We'll see when I show up for the flight.

I am accustomed to taking a carry on JanSport bag. I measured and it is larger than an allowed purse. In it I have meds, inhalers, underwear, a book, an extra pair of orthotics, cell phone charger, and a snack. That is what I am used to carrying on – free.

No dice with the discount airline. That'll be $45 please. That puts the cost of the flight at $253.

What about my clothes? Normally, I pay $25 to check one piece of luggage. Not on the discount airline. Another $42. So, we are up to $295. And this is all if I pay online in advance. Warning: prices may be higher at the airport.

No more discount airlines for me.

Socks

Recently I was shopping in Kohl's with my best friend, Penny. Actually, she was shopping. I had no money.

We came to the women's socks and I saw the kind I wear with slacks. They were in a pack of three, all black. I looked at them but, as I said, had no money. Penny offered to buy them for me. Sometimes I buy her things when we are shopping. We do that.

When I came home, I decided to keep them for school. I must tell you that I haven't bought socks for years, and most of mine are wearing out.

As I said, these are black. I need to find some denim ones to wear with jeans. I only have a few pair left, and they are getting thin and have holes.

There is a drawer in my dresser that is devoted to socks. The front row has the socks I currently wear. In the back are thinner socks that I wear with certain shoes. Thrown on top of those are some socks that I never matched.

The other day I decided to pull those out and match them. Well, this must be where all of Erma Bombeck's missing socks have gone. I had no idea there were so many socks in the back of the drawer.

They are mostly black, shades of black, and some navy. A few of the black had faded to charcoal grey. They were easy to match.

Have you ever tried to match socks that haven't seen their mates in years? I now have a large pile sitting on the dryer awaiting their union. Maybe I'll just dump them into the back of the drawer and let them rest in peace.

Staples

I haven't been able to staple papers for a couple of years because I thought I needed staples. This is one for the books. I just don't know which books.

Finally, the other day I was with a friend at Staples. While there, I decided to buy a pack of staples. Actually, I bought a double pack because it was so cheap.

Next on the list was to find my stapler. Actually, I have two of them. This proved to be less difficult than I imagined. The second cabinet I opened held not only both staplers, but a box of staples.

Never think something is lost in my house. It will be found eventually.

Actually, I think the reason I put them in the cabinet is they were collecting dust sitting on my desk.

I was so happy to be able to staple the two pages I had printed off the internet. It's the little things that matter.

Sylvia's Confusion

Last Friday, my friend Sylvia was in town running errands. She lives in a development several miles from town.

She called me and wanted to meet at McDonald's for a soda and chat a while. I was free so I went there. It's not far from my house.

We visited for a while. As we were leaving, she told me to get hold of Kay to meet for lunch the following week. Because of swim class, Sylvia's only free days are Wednesday and Friday. But she had plans on Friday, so that only left Wednesday.

I emailed Kay and asked if she could meet us at 1:00 at the Capital. Probably. She had some things going on in the morning.

So I got back to Sylvia. She thought she could work it out and would get back to me. Now, remember, she is the one who was only available on Wednesday. I reminded her of this.

Next she emailed and asked if we could meet at 11:30 so she could leave by 2:00. She had errands to run. I said OK and emailed Kay of the time change.

Later that evening, Sylvia called me and asked if we could meet at 12:00. Are you ready for this?

She wanted to drive into town and pay her hairdresser for blueberries and then drive back out to a hardware store and then drive back into town and meet at the restaurant.

I told her that made no logical sense and suggested she go to the hardware store first, then her hairdresser in town and then meet at the Capital. She said she'd figure it out.

Once again I emailed Kay of the time change. She did not respond.

I got there early and got our table. Sylvia arrived about 12:05. We ordered. Kay came in around 12:15 or so. She told Sylvia to get her act together next time.

Pillow Cases

Have you bought new sheets and pillow cases in the last ten years? Have you noticed the pillow cases are made for smaller pillows than you own?

The struggle is real. My cat tries to help, to no avail. I dread washing the bedclothes. Sometimes I wash them in the morning and wait until bedtime to put them back on. It's not the sheets I mind. It's the dreaded pillow cases.

Dealing with my pillow is the worst. It is memory foam. Trust me. It does not remember the pillow case.

They make pillow cases too narrow even for regular pillows. I don't get it. I have always bought standard sized pillows. There was no problem with pillow cases fitting in the past.

My best friend has found a remedy for this problem. She buys an extra flat sheet and makes her own pillow cases. I'm thinking of asking her to make pillow cases for me. I can just see the look on her face.

Laundry day – mine is every day – first you have to remove the pillow cases without tearing them. Good luck with that.

It's finally time to make the bed – or else

sleep on the bare mattress and pillows. You've waited as long as you can. You yank and shove and push and shake the pillow trying to get the pillow case on the pillow. It's enough to throw your back out. Ugh.

Pillow cases are just too narrow. What is wrong with the manufacturers? Don't they make their own beds?

Consumers revolt. Leave the pillow cases on the shelves and buy an extra sheet. Make or have someone make pillow cases for you. If no one buys pillow cases, maybe the manufacturers will get the message. Maybe.

Birds

Every day in the summer I argue with the birds. Every single day that I'm home.

There is a pretty little girl – tortoise shell cat – that I feed. In fact, she depends on me for food. In the winter, I try to fatten her up to keep her warm.

Last winter a friend's husband made a little shelter for her. She didn't use it.

Little Tortie is not the only one who eats the food I put out. I've seen other cats. Saw an orange cat last week. I don't want outside cats to go hungry.

They are not mine. I can't pet them. Little Tortie will talk to me, but even she keeps her distance.

Back to the birds. I buy Purina Cat Chow to feed Little Tortie and other stray cats. A 3.15 pound bag costs me $4.99. I don't mind. This is for the cats.

The birds think I am feeding them. Not on your life. I do not own a bird feeder. If I did, I would feel guilty because they would be easy prey for the cats.

Everyday I have to shake the bell on the door to get them away from the cat food dish.

Every single day. They just don't get the message.

And imagine how dirty they make the water dish. This water is for Little Tortie and other cats. Notice I said cats, not birds.

I have repeatedly told the birds the food is for the cats. I don't buy cat food to feed the birds.

Then there is the mess they make on my brick sidewalk. Do you think I appreciate that? Well, I do not.

They do, however, provide entertainment for my cat Mitzi who sits at the glass door and watches them. They aren't even afraid of her. I guess they know she can't get to them.

Oh, well. The daily argument with the birds continues.

Salt Caves

I just read a brochure from one of the local salt caves. We have two that I know of. I've actually been to the one. My daughter knows the owner and it is near my house.

The other one is not far from me, maybe a mile. The owner offered me a free session to get me to try it.

According to the brochure, salt cave therapy offers a wide variety of benefits. It reduces inflammation. Just what I need. This place offers a forty-five minute session. Today, I might need one an hour. Inflammation produces stiffness in the joints and muscles. I can barely move today. Sign me up for an all day session.

In the future, for prevention I'll need to sleep in the salt cave. They play soft music. I do that at home at night. May I bring my cat?

It supports immune function. After this past year, mine needs all the help it can get. Pneumonia three times. Seriously. Bronchitis, sinusitis. Better stay in the salt cave 24/7.

The brochure even says it acts as a natural disinfectant. Did you know that humans need to be disinfected? I did not know that.

It just goes to show you even a seventy-year

old can learn something new.

Sitting in a salt cave promotes more energy. I sure need that today. I'm about to fall asleep writing this. Do they deliver, energy, I mean? Let the nap begin.

Underwear

I recently found a couple of unopened packs of underwear on a shelf in my closet. Where did they come from? Then I remembered buying them at a Walmart in Washington state several years ago while visiting my daughter.

Each pack contains six pair. Brand new. Never opened. And here I've been wearing holey underwear for at least a year.

A male friend – widower – told me he has fifty pair of underwear. He has well water at his house which turns his clothes brown, so he has to go to the laundromat. Hope he doesn't drink the water. Is there such a thing as brown lung disease?

He goes to the laundromat once a month. Hence the need for a large supply of underwear.

I remember having to use the laundromat many years ago when I was working in malls. This was last century.

There was a D.E. Jones store in the local mall. When I needed a clean towel or wash cloth, I would just buy one at D.E. Jones. You can imagine the collection of towels I accumulated.

Now that I've found new packs of underwear,

I have a sufficient supply. And I can wash them at home.

Bras are a different story. The few that I have are left over from the turn of the century. I can remember when the turn of the century meant 1900. I wasn't alive back then, but we talked about it.

Ancient, frayed, worn out bras give little support. I wonder why I bother.

Actually, I bought a new bra last year. Same style and size as my others. I brought it home and guess what? They make them smaller now. When I returned it, I just got a refund. I did not have the heart to buy a bigger size.

Still with the worn out bras.

Summer Funds

Getting through the summer financially is not an easy task. Yes, I have a small pension and Social Security, but it's just not enough.

During the school year I substitute teach a few days a week. Near the end of the year, I aim for four or five days a week.

I had a perfect plan last year. I would work three days a week and save a large percentage of my pay. That savings would get me through the next summer, plus I'd have travel money.

Wonderful plan. It did not take into account three bouts of pneumonia, several bouts of bronchitis and sinusitis. Nope. By the third day of subbing, the plan was in the toilet. No savings.

Every summer I take out a small signature loan from my bank. That's how I normally get through the summer. This year I needed the loan in the spring because of a planned trip.

Along comes the middle of June and my living expenses are greater than my fixed income. Also, I need money for two trips and show rents.

After stewing over this for a couple of weeks, I apply online to a local loan company. The amount I apply for is less than their minimum, so I up the amount of my request.

Good news. I have been approved. I just have to call and speak with a local agent. So, I did.

She's very nice. Asks me four thousand questions and finally says they will approve me for a higher amount. OK. She gives me an appointment for the next morning.

Again, I have to answer more questions. She leaves and comes back a while later. Good news. I am approved for an even higher amount. Why not?

I sign my life away – actually my check book. The interest is about equal to the loan.

The next day the money is deposited into my account. I buy plane tickets, books to sell, vitamins to keep me going, pay a few bills, apply to a couple shows.

I also put $150 in savings which I will withdraw in a couple of weeks for my Seattle trip.

The good news, I'm told, is that in six months I can apply for more money. Summer is expensive. I'm putting my savings plan into effect once school starts. Maybe.

Inspired

Along the way, many of us have been inspired to write by other writers. Going back to younger days when I wrote poetry (yes, I still write poetry), I suppose I was inspired by Emily Dickinson, Walt Whitman, and the Book of Proverbs.

Moving on into my mid and late twenties, I was a great fan of Ernest Hemingway. I was intrigued by his sitting in the outdoor cafes of Paris writing.

Then there were two great humorists who captured my interest: James Thurber and Erma Bombeck. I remember sitting in bed at night reading their works and finding them enormously funny. My husband at the time was not impressed.

About twenty years ago, I found myself reading the humorous columns of Dave Barry.

Coming up to current times, the humorous duo of Lisa Scottoline and daughter Francesca Serritella have provided hours of entertainment and laughter for me. In terms of humorists, I think Bombeck and Scottoline top the list.

You see, writers must not only write. We must read as well. I understand that Dean

Koontz reads two hundred books a year. I have a ways to go to catch up.

Writers must read for pleasure as well as for knowledge. Our brains must stay active so that we can continue to write.

Responsibility and Consequences

My pastor preached about this subject yesterday. He talked about something I as a substitute teacher, could relate to. Let me elaborate.

A child caught in the act generally says, "I didn't do it."

As a substitute, I sometimes must tell students to stop talking. The response? You guessed it. They said they were not talking.

"But I watched you talking."

"No, it wasn't me." Often the student will get belligerent. At this point I find it better to drop the subject.

Do they think I'm blind? Stupid? Senile? It's a refusal to take responsibility for their actions. Are they not held accountable at home?

Let's go back a few years – more than a few. I was under six years of age because we moved when I was six.

As a child, I liked to get up early. Very early. My grandmother liked to sleep in. My mother also preferred to sleep in. All these years later and I still like mornings. Afternoons are for sleeping.

Back to my story. I would get up very early,

dress and go outside to swing or play. On this one particular morning, I got tired of waiting for my grandmother to get up. I guess I didn't like being alone.

I picked up a small rock and threw it through a window. That woke my grandmother. She raised the window and yelled at me.

My reaction: "I didn't do it." There was no one else around.

Responsibility and consequences. I don't remember the consequences, but I'm sure there must have been some.

Toe

I have a sore toe. It's the big toe on my left foot. Shoes aggravate it. Walking is not fun.

How did it get sore? Are you ready for this?

My cat, Mitzi, loves me and has to be where I am, except in the shower. She waits outside, but close.

On Saturday morning, I stepped out of the shower and Mitzi was lying in the front of her food dish which is just outside my walk-in closet.

Seeing that I had survived the shower, she decided to eat. I dried off and headed for my walk-in closet to get dressed.

Do you remember one of the laws of physics that says two objects cannot occupy the same space at the same time? This law contributed to my sore toe.

Just as I stepped behind Mitzi, she decided to move, thereby stepping on my foot. One of her back claws punctured the area beside the nail on my big toe. Yelp!

She was horrified. I could tell by her expression that she felt bad for hurting Mommy.

I applied Bacitracin, put on my socks, dressed and went about my day. Aware that my toe hurt.

Imagine my surprise that night when I took my socks off and saw that the whole side of my toe was bright red. I'm diabetic and don't want to lose my toe or foot or leg.

Out came the basin and a box of salt that has been in the cupboard for a couple of years. I rarely use salt. Probably bought it the last time my sister visited, a couple of years ago.

Well, I soaked my foot and then poured peroxide on my toe and went to bed convinced that I would seek medical treatment after church.

In the morning, some of the redness was gone. I checked it after church and decided to wait and see if it continued to improve.

It's Monday morning and there is less redness. Maybe I'll soak it again this evening. We'll see what tomorrow brings.

It's still sore and I'm watching it. I don't want to be an alarmist, but I'll keep an eye on it.

I told this story to my daughter. Her reaction: "Sometimes I have no words."

Eyeglass Case

A simple thing. At least it used to be. Let me explain.

For years – many, many years – I used soft cloth cases. No problem. I had one for my regular glasses and one for my prescription sunglasses. I kept them in my purse. Perfect.

Then things changed. As a substitute, I often have to cover another class during my free period. Instead of carrying my lunch bag everywhere, I started putting my water bottle in my purse.

The first casualty from this was my sunglasses. The frame broke. They were able to fit the lenses into another frame. Still costly.

About six months later my regular frame broke in half. I was not happy. This pair was a gift from my daughter a number of years ago. I'm not good about regular eye exams. I've been thinking about getting an exam for a couple of years, but my family doctor says I have to wait until my blood sugar normalizes. We'll see how long that takes.

Well, after having to spend money for a second pair of frames, I got smart. I got hard cases for them. They are cumbersome and add weight to my purse which is already heavy.

While she was home earlier in the summer, my daughter bought me a nice Thirty-One case from our cousin. It's padded , so my glasses should be fine.

Did I tell you I have a large wallet and an appointment book in my purse?

Yesterday, I put my glasses on to drive and the left side is too close to my eye. Guess I'll have to have them adjusted. Who knows how many times I'll have to go back until they are right.

Today, I started the search for my hard black case. Unable to find it, I found a second brown case. Now, I'll have two brown cases in my purse and will just have to open each one to find the right pair of glasses.

Water and Blood Work

I have procrastinated as long as I can. Today is Tuesday. My doctor's appointment is next Monday. She wants blood work done before she sees me. That way she'll know how bad I've been.

My original plan was to have it done Monday morning (yesterday). The problem : I forgot to hydrate (drink water) on Sunday. Oh, I probably consumed half a bottle. The rest of the day I drank Coke – Coke Zero these days. That actually dehydrates a person.

I have tiny veins, so it really is necessary for me to drink lots of water to increase the blood volume.

No blood work on Monday. Once again I failed to hydrate. This time I drank iced tea and Coke. Now, Tuesday is out.

Today is Tuesday. In order for my doctor to have all my blood work results on Monday, I really must have my blood drawn tomorrow.

How am I doing so far? Three fourths of a bottle of water down. It has to mix with the tea and Coke Zero.

My goal for today is three bottles of water and then one in the morning. I'm on deadline.

We'll see if I make it.

Again With the Blood Work

Today is the day. I got up, showered, dressed, fed Mitzi and the outside cat. I had nothing to eat or drink except water.

My biggest decision was whether to go to the hospital lab or Summit Health. I live halfway in between.

So, I get my purse, water bottle and book bag (I read while waiting) and left the house. On Walker Road, I turned toward the hospital. My car made the decision.

At the hospital, I found a place to park, got out of the car and walked toward the entrance. Crap. No paper. I had forgotten the lab slip.

I walked back to the car, got in and drove home to get the paper. This time when I got to Walker Road, I turned toward Summit Health. Maybe it's a better choice today.

After parking the car, I walked into the lab waiting room, signed in and sat down. No book bag. I had left it in the car. Well, I wasn't going back outside, so I would just have to sit and meditate.

My wait was not too long. Fortunately the lab tech was able to access my vein without any difficulty. Done.

Now to decide on breakfast.

How to Waste Time

Are you good at wasting time? I am. In fact, I excel at it. They should give awards for proficiency in wasting time. I would have a wall full. Or maybe a room.

A good way to waste time is to become a TV junkie. Wow! I've got that one covered. I can watch re-runs of shows over and over and over. I am still mesmerized by them. Can you believe I still want to know what happens next when I've seen the show fourteen times? Yep. TV junkie. I'll take an award for that.

Then there's email. How many of you have to check your email thirty-two times an hour – just in case? That's another award for my wall.

I feed a stray or feral cat. Naturally, I have to look out the door at least every ten minutes to see if she is there or if there is food in her dish. That reminds me. I should put fresh water in her bowl.

My cat Mitzi naps most of the afternoon. She has a favorite box in the bedroom. Don't ask. Of course, I have to check on her at least forty times. Naturally, I rub her head. She grunts because I have disturbed her.

Now comes the big one – Facebook. Give me

three awards for this. Think I'll go check it now.

Or you could just wander around the house doing nothing. You could open the refrigerator door to look for food that wasn't there five minutes ago.

So many ways to waste time. I'm sure you have your own unique ways. Guess it's time to go meet a friend for tea.

Oh, I almost forgot one – the inevitable nap time.

Trip to the Market

It had been several years since Heather and I had been to Pike Place Market in Seattle. Since I liked it so much, she decided we would visit it on this trip to the Pacific Northwest.

The main artery that connects to every town is the I-5. Riding in the car going to and from Seattle always made me a nervous wreck. This time was no different except that it was worse. The traffic was at least five times heavier than it was on any other trip.

Heather remarked how much she hated traveling on the I-5. I just sat there ready to have apoplexy at any moment.

Eventually we made it to Seattle. Trying to find a parking space was also a nightmare. We made our way to the lot where we always parked. It was full. On the second trip around the lot, we found a parking space. Bless the person who vacated it. The parking fee was outrageous.

My daughter informed me I needed to have a very good time because she wasn't coming back here again.

I have never seen so many people at the Market. You would have thought it was a holiday. It was only a regular Thursday, not even a weekend.

Heather loves seeing the fresh flowers at the Market. I love looking at the cards and pictures at a stand near the entrance. I always buy cards. One year I bought a framed picture. Heather also bought one for me. I have them hanging in my house.

The wall to wall people was suffocating, so we went outside and walked past the outdoor vendors and crossed the street to look at the shops there. One of the shops is a German deli. I've always wanted to try their cooked sausage. Today, I did. It was very good.

We wanted a cinnamon donut, but the line was so long neither of us wanted to stand in it.

One shop had delicious mac and cheese. We waited in that line so Heather could get a cup. That was her lunch.

It was time to leave the city and join the millions of people on the I-5. Time for me to be a nervous wreck again.

Centralia Outlets

We checked out of the hotel and decided to go to Centralia shopping. This meant another trip on the I-5. Just entering the entrance ramp today proved to be a major accomplishment.
There was a car sitting in the way of the entrance ramp. Heather's reaction was priceless.
"Get out of the way. I have traffic to sit in."
And so we inched our way to Centralia.
Shopping proved productive today. I can't remember if we ate first or shopped first. But we found a fabulous restaurant with home cooked food. It was on the perimeter of the shopping center.
Country Cousins was an interesting looking restaurant that I found inviting. The inside was replete with local artifacts. There was even a small gift area near the cashier.
The restaurant was fairly busy, but we were fortunate enough to get a booth. The area where we were seated had a large party, so the waitress did not get to us right away, which gave us time to look over the menu.
When the waitress came to our booth, I had a million questions for her. Well, I had never been there. Heather hid behind her menu.

After our waitress brought our drinks, I had more questions. By this time, I think Heather wanted to escape through the window. She had made her selection – the roast turkey dinner. I was the hold up.

Finally, I chose the small portion of pot roast, complete with red potatoes, carrots, onions and gravy.

When our meals arrived, I was so glad I ordered the small portion. It was large enough to feed two people. And delicious. Both of our meals were delicious.

Time to get back on the I-5 and head to our next destination.

Coffee at 3 AM

Penny and her husband recently took a four day trip to visit Ron's family. They left on Friday morning to visit his sister, who is a widow, in Ohio. She had called on Thursday evening wondering where they were because she had prepared dinner, and it was waiting for them. Just a day early.

Their next stop was upstate PA to visit his sister and brother-in-law. They had a good time there. On Sunday morning they all went to breakfast at a place called The Train Station. It was quaint and the food was good.

Eventually, they made their way to the Erie area to visit with his brother and sister-in-law. Here's where things get a bit interesting.

After dinner, ice cream and visiting, they all turned in for the night, probably around midnight. Well, at some point Penny got up to use the bathroom. It's an older bladder thing.

On the way to the bathroom, she saw a light from the TV in the living room and smelled coffee brewing. Since she did not know what time it was, she thought it must be morning. If coffee was brewing, they would probably start cooking breakfast soon.

Maybe Penny should get in the shower. Since she was still tired, she put out a towel and wash cloth for Ron and went back to bed. The clock said 3 AM.

When she got up around 7 AM, she learned that Ron's brother often gets up in the middle of the night, watches TV and drinks a cup of coffee. Then he goes back to bed.

Penny was glad she had not showered at 3 AM.

Old School

Several years ago, a friend brought a short article to church for me to read. It pictured a typewriter – an older model. The article talked about Danielle Steele writing her books on a typewriter instead of a computer. I thought that was pretty neat.

Today, while subbing, I met an eleventh grade boy who is an author. He was reading his own book.

The cover intrigued me, so I asked to see the book. When I saw it was edited by a teacher at the school, I was surprised. That's when he told me he is the author. He also told me he's working on another one. He published through amazon.

Then, he opened his notebook to show me his current writing. He creates on paper with pen. That's how his brain works. He can't create at the computer. He said teachers are always telling him to write on the computer, but he can't create that way. He has to write on paper.

Guess what. I am the same way. I couldn't believe that a sixteen year old's brain works the same way as this seventy year old's.

I'm going to order his book from amazon. I

want to encourage him.

He hand writes on paper. In today's world, we are a unique breed.

Drug Costs

My friend Penny is diabetic. She has been on Invokana for a long time. Her doctor wanted to switch her to injectable Trulicity. I personally have had good results with it. So far Penny has not.

Her co-pay for Invokana was $60. She decided to refill her prescription since her blood sugar is now over 300.

She is on Medicare and has hit the donut hole. Her Invokana co-pay is now $150 for one month. Not affordable.

Why are the drug companies in the U.S. so greedy? What is a person supposed to do?

I dread getting my Trulicity filled. My co-pay is $75 a month. Who knows what it will be when I hit the donut hole. This makes no sense. None.

We are not alone. Thousands of senior citizens in the U.S. go through this each year. I'll bet Congressmen and Senators don't have this problem. And we are the ones still working and paying their outrageous salaries.

How Rumors Get Started

This is a simple communication breakdown, but it illustrates how easy it can be to repeat false information.

My cousin sells Thirty-One. She posted the picture of a tote that could be used as a large purse. Both my daughter and I liked it. Heather commented and asked the price. This was on Facebook.

My cousin said the price was $72.

I asked if the plaid portion of the tote was vinyl or fabric. She said it was fabric.

I told her I might have to see it at some point. I really meant smell it because you already know about my scent/chemical allergies.

She said to go to her web site and look up Cindy's Tote. I asked what her web site was and she said she didn't have one.

I told her I gave up mine a few years ago because I didn't think it was cost effective. I got an order now and then, but that was all.

She asked, "You had one?"

I said yes, for my books It was judywalter.com.

She said she thought I meant I had the purse. She then posted the link to her Thirty-

One web site.
See what I mean? Confusion.

Hot Dogs

I have two Nathan's hot dogs cooking on the stove. I was thinking about eating them. I was visualizing biting into the hot dog bun. Alas, I bought bread, not hot dog buns, thinking of toast in the morning. Oh, well.

Too Short

After looking at one of the pictures of me at the St. Paul Authors' Fair, I've decided I'm too short. If I were taller, I wouldn't look so fat. So you see, I just need to stretch myself and become taller. Then I will look thinner. Weight problem solved.

Judy S. Walter is a retired high school English teacher. As an author, she has written and published more than eleven books in a variety of genre. This is her third book of humorous stories.

Walter has written a series of books about individual cats. They are popular with all ages.

She sells her books at cat shows, craft shows, book festivals, at signings, in stores and libraries, and on amazon.com.

Walter resides in PA.

Other Books by Judy S. Walter

I love Bacon

Memories of a High School Teacher

Nightmare in Europe

Sammy, The Talking Cat

Sammy Goes On Tour

The Grey and White Stranger

Life With Mitzi

The Dog From York and Other Stories

Simple Book Marketing

The Escape Artist -
A collection of Poems and Essays

Made in the USA
Middletown, DE
13 January 2025

68772188R00057